A *FALCON* GUIDE®

BACKPACKING TIPS
Trail-tested Wisdom from FalconGuide Authors

Second Edition

*Edited by Russ Schneider and Bill Schneider
with contributions from 13 FalconGuide Authors*

FALCON®

GUILFORD, CONNECTICUT
HELENA, MONTANA
AN IMPRINT OF THE GLOBE PEQUOT PRESS

AFALCONGUIDE®

Copyright © 2005 by The Globe Pequot Press
A previous edition of this book was published by Falcon Publishing,
Inc. in 1998.

Text design by Lisa Reneson
Illustrations by Todd Telander

Library of Congress Cataloging-in-Publication Data is available.

Backpacking tips : trail-tested wisdom from FalconGuide authors /
edited by Russ Schneider and Bill Schneider, with contributions
from 13 FalconGuide authors. — 2nd ed.
      p. cm. — (A Falcon guide)
   ISBN 0-7627-3747-6
   1. Backpacking. 2. Hiking. I. Title: Back packing tips. II. Schneider,
Russ, 1972- III. Schneider, Bill. IV. Series.
GV199.6.B34 2005
796.51—dc22   2004060850

Manufactured in the United States of America
Second Edition/First Printing

CONTENTS

PREFACE AND ACKNOWLEDGMENTS

The first edition of *Backpacking Tips* was the first book project I officially worked on with my dad, and although I did not see it at the time, it was a great opportunity. It took many years, losing my father-in-law to a head-on collision, and spending time with my own son to realize that few people get the chance to work so closely with their father—and put a little food on the plate, too.

These opportunities are fewer and farther between today. Consolidation in the outdoor guidebook industry (and publishing industry in general) eventually led to Falcon being combined with The Globe Pequot Press and Bill stepping back to semiretirement and returning to his writing roots. While researching this edition, I paged through a tall stack of hiking guidebooks written by my father. I found gems and trail humor sprinkled through mountains of fact. In it all was a love for heading down the trail with family and friends, something I am proud to say he passed on.

The first edition of this book also included broad participation of many other FalconGuide authors. The author network is not as close-knit these days. Hence, we decided rather than let this gem of a book go out of print, we would breathe new life into it. We have added many tips compiled from the many guidebooks we have written and the experience of all the back-packing trips we have guided, including my nine seasons as a backpacking guide with Glacier Wilderness Guides in Glacier National Park and Bill's twelve years leading Yellowstone Institute courses on Hiking and Camping in Grizzly Country.

Special thanks to all of the FalconGuide authors for contributing tips to the first edition of *Backpacking Tips,* including: Ron Adkison, Donna Ikenberry, Polly Burke, Bill Cunningham, Bert Gildart, Jane Gildart, Bill Hunger, Bruce Grubbs, Rhonda Ostertag, George Ostertag, Will Harmon, Gilbert Preston, and Fred Barstad. It is amazing how timeless their on-trail advice truly is. The FalconGuide brand continues to be *the* name in outdoor guidebooks. The tips in this book are only a small portion of the FalconGuide body of outdoor knowledge. If you are hungry for more, pick up a few of their books, listed in the back of this book.

— *Russ Schneider*

A FEW WORDS ABOUT ULTRALIGHT BACKPACKING

Most people tend to carry more weight in their back-packs than necessary, but sometimes this is a good thing.

Ultralight backpacking equipment is the craze, but in some cases these efforts sacrifice safety. And safety always comes first. This is especially true when hiking in northern-tier mountain ranges, where it can be winter on *any* summer day.

When deciding what to put in your backpack, think winter. Say to yourself: "If I were caught in an early-season snowstorm for twenty-four hours of freezing rain, would I be able to stay warm—and alive?"

With desert hiking, you have more opportunities to lighten your pack by leaving home certain items, but in northern-tier states there are some essential items, such as a good tent (not a poncho that doubles as a tent!), reliable rain gear (both coat and pants, not an umbrella!), stove and fuel, and enough warm clothes to

survive a winter storm or dip in an icy river. I keep one set of clothes double-bagged for emergencies. I call them "dry clothes" and never, ever, under any circumstances let them get wet. On most trips I don't even use these clothes, but on the few occasions I have used them, they have been worth their weight in gold—and definitely worth the extra pound in my backpack.

There is nothing wrong with spending the extra money for ultralight gear, but make sure it's reliable. What good is a two-ounce raincoat that doesn't keep you dry or a two-pound tent the wind blows away?

In addition to safety, there is the issue of comfort. You can leave everything home except essential items, but I personally go backpacking to enjoy myself. I always opt for lighter models, of course, but I take such things as binoculars, a camera, fly-fishing gear, and a book. I could leave all these items home and have a safe trip, but instead I prefer to have a safe and enjoyable trip, even if it isn't ultralight.

— *Bill Schneider*

THE TIPS

Words to Live By

■ The Boy Scouts of America have been guided for decades by what is perhaps the single best piece of safety advice—Be prepared! For starters, this means carrying survival and first-aid materials, proper clothing, a compass, and a topographic map, and knowing how to use them.

■ Tell somebody where you are going and when you plan to return. File your "flight plan," including alternatives and which car you are taking (with license plate number), with a friend or relative before taking off, and call that person immediately upon your return.

■ Before you head into the backcountry, highlight your route on a map and leave it with a friend or at a local ranger station. —*Will Harmon*

Planning

■ Have several backup trips lined up within the region of your intended trek. This allows you to alter your hike based on weather, insect, and trail or road conditions. If you expect rain, take the hike up a forested valley; if mosquitoes are voracious, hike a dry peak. —*Rhonda and George Ostertag*

■ Pick a hike appropriate to your level of experience. Beginners should try a short overnighter before attempting an extended trip. Try to keep your first trip to about 5 miles or less one-way.

■ Check with the land-management agency to make sure your route follows maintained trails; if so, find out when the trail was last cleared of downfall. Unmaintained trails with lots of downfall make travel slower, more strenuous, and sometimes dangerous. If you anticipate hiking off-trail or on a trail that has not been maintained for years, expect slow going and difficult route-finding.

■ Engage all participants in picking and planning a hike. For a happier group, each individual should be invited to provide input on length, terrain, and duration. —*Polly Burke*

■ The prime season for hiking in most of North America is mid-July through September. Hungry mosquitoes and blackflies await hikers in most areas in June and even into July. In addition, with the deep snowfall in the high country, you can't hike many high-altitude trails until mid-July; and in some low-altitude areas, trails remain wet and mushy, and high water makes fords dangerous until then. Southern states and desert areas offer great hiking in early spring and early fall, so if you are willing to travel, you can hike almost year-round.

■ For early-spring trips, seek out trails at lower

elevations on south-facing slopes. These areas shed their snow and dry out earlier than other areas.
—*Will Harmon*

Conditioning

■ Hiking and backpacking are by their very nature strenuous outdoor activities. Consult a physician before going on a backpacking trip.

■ Start with a very short backpack trip your first time out.

■ Try easy hikes with your pack fully loaded to get in shape before you try extended treks.

■ A combination of weight training, exercise machines, and running or cross-country skiing during the winter months can help you get in shape for hiking season.

■ Put fifty pounds in your pack and walk a mile around the local high school track. Walk 2 miles the next week, and so on, until you feel comfortable with your fitness level.

Guidebooks and Maps

■ Half the fun of planning a backpacking trip is poring over maps, finding the most remote places, and dreaming about visiting them.

■ Buy a guidebook on the area you plan to visit early in the planning stages of your trip. It may help you decide which hike you want to take, not just what the trail will be like when you get there. Maps printed in guidebooks are general locator maps only and have limited value. Be sure to bring topographic or agency maps.

■ Guidebooks can help you locate an area you want to visit and provide detailed trip-planning and trail descriptions, but a guidebook doesn't take the place of a good topographic map, compass, and GPS and knowing how to use them.

■ Many topographic maps are outdated. While these maps are still accurate in topography, years of logging and other development can change the surface of the land. Updated guidebooks and information from local management agencies offer the most accurate guidelines. —*Bill Hunger*

■ United States Geological Survey (USGS) 7.5-minute topographic, Trails Illustrated, Green Trails, and Earthwalk Press are the best general maps to carry. The USDA Forest Service (USDAFS) or Bureau of Land Management (BLM) recreation maps may be the only maps with road numbers and exact trailhead locations for a particular area.

■ Consider purchasing a MapTech or Topo! CD-

Rom containing all the topographic maps for your state or favorite national park. This allows you to instantly print out as many copies as you like of your chosen route. Visit www.maptech.com for more info.

■ You can find USGS, USDAFS, BLM, and Canadian topographic maps at many sporting goods stores or at visitor centers in the area you visit. Inquire with local management agencies about other available maps, but you should always have some type of topographic map.

■ You can order topographic maps directly from the USGS and Canada Map Office at the following addresses:

USGS Information Services
Federal Center
P.O. Box 25286
Denver, CO 80225
(800) ASK–USGS (800–275–8747)
http://geography.usgs.gov

Center for Topographic Information
Natural Resources Canada
615 Booth Street, Room 75
Ottawa, Ontario
Canada K1A0E9
(800) 465–6277
http://maps.nrcan.gc.ca

■ Be realistic about estimating mileage on a map. Trails are never straight, even if they appear so.

Types of Trips

■ Loop trips start and finish at the same trailhead, with no (or very little) retracing of your steps.

■ Out-and-back trips take you to a destination and then back to the trailhead. They are logistically simple but limit the amount of scenery.

■ Base camp trips involve hiking into an area, setting up camp in the same place for several days, and taking shorter day trips from camp. This allows for enjoyable fishing, climbing, and day hiking in remote areas. Plan a long first day of hiking to a location that offers a variety of intriguing day trips.

■ Shuttle trips are point-to-point hikes that require two vehicles (one left at both ends of the trail) or a prearranged pickup at a designated time and place.

■ When avoiding a car shuttle by doing a one-way hike in two groups, each party should carry keys to both cars. Bad weather or unforeseen problems may prevent a midtrip key swap. Agree on a post-trip meeting point ahead of time. —*Bruce Grubbs*

Permits

■ Backcountry use regulations help preserve the natural landscape and protect visitors. Many national parks, state parks, and, increasingly, national forests require that you obtain a permit before camping in popular areas.

■ Take advantage of advance reservation systems to get the best sites, but expect to pay a small fee for that permit. If you cannot get a permit in advance, you can usually get one at a visitor center in the area you are visiting, but it might not be for your most preferred campsite.

■ Use the Internet to search for information on your destination, especially regarding fees, permits, and special regulations, which often change yearly.

■ In addition to backcountry campsite permits, many areas now charge fees for parking at popular trailheads.

Equipment

■ Don't get too caught up in the gear. Too much expensive gear can break your checkbook, and heavy high-tech gadgets can break your back. Spend money on rain gear (7 to 9 percent of your gear weight), a good tent (10 to 14 percent), backpack (10 to 15 percent), and a warm sleeping bag (9 to 11 percent). Otherwise, moderately priced items will suffice.

■ Always test gear before buying it. Many outdoor-equipment stores offer rental programs so that you can make a test run.

■ Buy backpacks and boots from a shop that can fit you properly.

■ Search the Internet for online product reviews of gear you want to purchase before spending the money.

■ It is not really that special, but one piece of equipment you definitely need is a good supply of ziplock plastic bags. This handy invention is perfect for keeping food smell to a minimum and helps keep food from spilling on your pack, clothing, or other gear.

■ Online deals may seem great, but check prices locally first. You may get just as good a price on a quality backpack at your local outdoor specialty store as online. In addition, you will get a proper fit and service.

Survival Kit

■ Carry a survival kit that includes a compass, whistle, matches in a waterproof container, cigarette lighter, candles, signal mirror, flashlight, fire starter, iodine tablets, and space blanket; Bill recommends a flare.

■ For the emergency fire-starting portion of your survival kit, we prefer regular matches in a good waterproof container to "waterproof" matches. It is a good idea to rip a piece of the strike strip off of the match box and stuff it in the jar too, so that you aren't looking for a dry rock in a wet snowstorm. This container should only be for true emergencies. For everyday use, place cigarette lighters in multiple gear bags so that you always have one handy—in your spice kit, with your pans, in the stuff sack you keep your stove in, in the top of your pack, and in your survival kit.

■ If you have a fancy butane emergency lighter, make it part of your survival kit; store it in a plastic bag with some artificial fire starter. This tip comes from river experience. If you really need to start a fire fast, grabbing the tightly sealed bag with the bomber butane lighter and some white fire starter sure can save the day.

■ To defend against hypothermia, stay dry and always maintain at least some emergency dry clothes in a waterproof stuff sack and garbage bag deep in your backpack. Avoid cotton clothing, which loses about 90 percent of its insulating value when wet. Choose clothes that provide good protection against wind and rain.

Food

■ You can make your trip much less enjoyable by fretting too much over food. Perhaps the most common option is freeze-dried food. It carries little smell and comes in convenient envelopes that allow you to cook it by merely adding boiling water. This means you don't have cooking pans to wash or store.

■ Bring high-energy snacks for day hiking. For overnight trips, don't burden yourself with too much heavy food; you can always look forward to a big steak in a restaurant on the drive home. Freeze-dried foods are light, but regular noodles and sauce work just fine. Plan your regular meals and then pack either one extra meal or one large extra bag of snacks. This isn't as important if you're traveling alone, but in a large group, running out of food can make everyone grumpy and miserable.

■ It is a good idea to split up your snacks into smaller portions. A huge bag of gorp at the top of someone's pack can really off-balance his or her load.

■ Dry prepacked meals (often pasta or rice based) offer an affordable alternative to freeze-dried foods. You can supplement these meals with pita bread, bagels, tortillas, and dehydrated salsa. Do not bring salt; most backpacking food contains plenty.

■ Take plenty of snacks. If you don't bring enough other food, you'll have something to keep you going.

■ Get calories from the following sources: 40 percent from carbohydrates, 30 percent from protein, and 30 percent from fat. On trips above 10,000 feet, you should increase your carbohydrate intake to 70 percent of your calories. —*Gilbert Preston, M.D.*

■ Make a tasty backpacking dinner by filling burrito shells with couscous or tabbouleh. Add some fresh vegetables on the first and second nights, and eat like a king or queen. —*Donna Ikenberry*

■ If you are heavily into extended backpacking trips, consider purchasing a food dehydrator. You should be able to recoup the cost by not having to purchase expensive, commercially available dehydrated foods. —*Bert and Jane Gildart*

■ Avoid fresh fruit and canned meats and fish when camping in bear country.

■ When not camping in bear country, a can of salmon, cream-cheese packets, a small jar of capers, and garlic bagels make a great lunch.

■ Fresh baguettes, picked up right before you hit the trailhead, make any sausage-and-cheese lunch better.

■ On extended trips, purposely pack one meal that is larger than needed (i.e., twice what you expect to eat in an average meal) and save it for later in the trip, when you are sure to eat it all.

Stoves

■ If you generally camp in mild climates, consider using butane canister stoves. They light easily, burn hot, and are lightweight.

■ If you plan to hike and camp in areas with colder temperatures with the possibility of summer snow, it is probably better to use a white-gas stove. Technology may make butane stoves more usable at colder temperatures, and it may be possible in the future to forgo white gas–burning stoves. However, using white gas arguably produces less wasted metal canisters than butane.

■ We have regularly used MSR Whisperlight and Optimus Expedition. Whisperlight stoves are hard to simmer on and harder to light correctly for most people. Optimus, at least the more reliable Optimus Expedition version, is good but also very heavy for a stove and makes sense only for a large group. We use the Coleman Peak 1, which is inexpensive, reliable, and easy to fix.

■ Regardless of what stove you purchase, the most important thing you need to know is how to use it.

After you purchase a stove, take it apart, put it back together, and see if you can purchase replacement parts. Start it, clean it, repair it, and light it prior to leaving home on every trip. You can make most stoves work if you keep them clean and maintained and know how to fix them. You may have to rebuild all or part of a stove after a while. This is especially true of shaker-jet models.

■ Follow starting directions exactly. If it says "pump twenty-five times," pump twenty-five times. Take the instructions with you on every trip.

■ If you can get away with it space-wise, it is nice to store your stove inside the pans; always have an extra cigarette lighter in there, too.

■ Remember that fuel canisters are not allowed on airplanes (just like bear spray), so check that the fuel for your stove can be purchased locally or on the drive to the trailhead.

■ Make sure multiple members of the group know how to start and operate the stove.

Cook Kits

■ Pack cooking utensils, a scrubby, soap, matches with strike strip (or cigarette lighters), and a food screen in the cook kit so that you always have them handy, such as inside the cooking pans.

■ If you plan to cook pancakes, do not use the lid of your aluminum cook kit. Carry a lightweight non-stick pan, or consider a different breakfast.

■ Bring a screen to filter food chunks out of dishwater before broadcasting it at least 100 feet away from water. Put food scraps in the garbage and pack it out.

■ It is nice to have one small pan and lid designated for hot water/drinks so that in between cooking meals you can keep the hot drinks flowing and make the most efficient use of a hot burner—saving fuel versus having to relight all the time. If you take only one pan to reduce weight, this won't be possible.

Clothing

■ Do not leave home without essential clothing for cold weather, even if the forecast looks good. The two most essential items are a rain suit and an extra wool sweater or fleece jacket. Other items are a little less important depending upon the climate, the length of your stay, the season, and the distance back to your vehicle. It is easy to carry too much, but it can be deadly to carry too little.

■ Although they are on the expensive side, a good lightweight rain jacket and rain pants and even a rain hat may be the best way to spend your back-packing dollar. A cheap backpack or wool sweater or even a pair of well-worn sneakers are better places to save money than on your survival suit. Good, light, breathable rain gear can allow you to enjoy the beauty of a wet snowstorm in July or a trip through an old-growth rain forest along the coast. In contrast, making a trip in cheap or poorly constructed rain gear or relying on an umbrella could get you killed in a bad storm. Your survival kit is for emergencies; don't be creating one.

■ Once you reach the top of a climb, take off the sweat-soaked layer of clothing directly next to your skin and replace it with a dry layer.

■ You might think that Polarfleece is lighter than wool. This is not always true. When we weighed a wool sweater and a fleece jacket of the same size and thickness, there was less than an ounce difference. However, if both get wet, the fleece will be lighter and will dry faster.

■ For desert hiking areas, strive for light, white cotton shirts, pants, and hats, but remember to bring warm clothing for the nighttime. Clear desert skies do not hold the daytime warmth.

■ When packing your clothes, remember to place your varied layers where you can get them easily. The Polarfleece doesn't do you any good if it is at the bottom of your pack and is too much trouble to get to. —*Polly Burke*

Shoes and Boots

■ Don't start down the trail with brand-new boots; thoroughly break in your boots before hitting the trail.

■ The best advice for dealing with blisters is to prevent them. Start with properly fitted boots that are really broken in. Once you know where your rub spots are, place slick tape, either duct or athletic, on high rub areas of your foot. Check frequently for "hot spots" while on the trail, and apply slick tape or moleskin as needed to reduce rubbing. Be careful with duct tape; some people swear by it, but it can pull off your skin if you are not careful.

■ Trail-running or trail-hiking shoes are low impact, light on your feet, and cheaper to replace than full leather boots. However, weak, injury-prone ankles may fare better with the stability of a full leather boot.

■ Hike your shoes dry to prevent them from shrinking.

■ Consider wearing waterproof, breathable socks

and running shoes for wet hiking. Any boot, no matter how expensive, will not protect your feet from wetness in heavy rain.

■ Always bring extra socks.

■ If your boots start to leak in bad weather, or you are using lightweight boots or running shoes that are not waterproof, use a couple of plastic bags as outer socks, and put your shoes on over them to help keep your feet dry. Leave the bags loose over your toes so that you will not punch holes in them. Gallon-size ziplock plastic bags work well.
—*Bruce Grubbs*

Tents

■ Practice setting up your tent in the backyard or your living room before you go backpacking so that you will not have to struggle with unfamiliar seams, poles, and stakes in pouring rain.

■ Tents are a big portion of both the weight and expense of backpacking. Cheap tents can make for a miserable and dangerous experience, while expensive tents usually are not worth the price. We do not recommend single-wall tents. You are better off sleeping under a well-strung tarp.

■ Four-season tents are often four pounds heavier than suitable three-season tents. Even if you think that you might use your tent all four seasons, you might want an additional, lighter tent in summer.

■ Get a freestanding or dome tent that requires few tent stakes. Tent stakes have a tendency to disappear, and you should be able to set up a tent without them.

■ Get a tent with a fly that completely protects all entrances and windows and preferably with a good vestibule or awning for dry storage outside the tent.

■ Get a stuff sack that is much larger than the size of the rolled-up tent. This speeds packing time and prevents wear and tear from shoving a too-large rolled up tent into a too-small stuff sack.

■ A lightweight nylon tarp can also be a survival item. It can be quickly erected to protect from rain, hail, sleet, and snow. —*Bert and Jane Gildart*

■ Take your rain gear into the tent at night so that you'll be prepared if you wake up to rain.

■ Always put the zippers at the top of the arch in the tent so that everybody can find them in the dark without turning on a flashlight.

■ Make sure everybody in the tent knows where the

flashlight and bear pepper spray are located so that everybody can find these items in the dark.

Sleeping Bags and Pads

■ A sleeping bag is a good place to lay down some extra dollars. It could save your life. Synthetic sleeping bags tend to be a little heavier than down-filled bags. Synthetic bags will, however, retain insulating value when wet, while down-filled bags will not. We recommend a 20 degree Fahrenheit bag or warmer. You can always cool off by unzipping the bag or sleeping on top.

■ To assure that your sleeping bag stays dry in any weather, heavy-duty garbage bags make excellent liners for sleeping bag stuff sacks. Place the plastic bag inside your stuff sack, and then stuff the sleeping bag inside and close with a twist tie after fully compressing the bag. *—Fred Barstad*

■ For a pillow, stuff some clothes into your sleeping bag stuff sack, and then zip your fleece vest or jacket around the outside of your makeshift pillow. This gives you a comfy pillow that is fluffy and soft on your face.

■ Rolling up a Therma-Rest Therma-Lounger Crazy Creek–type chair/mattress, step by step. The key is to roll the air mattress toward the open nozzle so that you gradually push the air out as you roll. After you have made a tight roll, take in the opposite direction, clicking the quick release around the tight roll. Cinch it down with the quick-release strap. After you roll it up tight, remember to close the nozzle so that the heating of the sun does not suck air in.

■ Leaving your air mattress in the sun will partially inflate it, but to make it hard enough to sleep on, you will most likely need to use your lungs.

Backpacks

■ Size matters. Do not buy a too-big pack; it will just induce you to carry more than you need.

■ We recommend internal-frame packs. External-frame packs are suited to big-shouldered people. Internal-frame packs put the weight on your hips, where most of us have the big muscles.

■ Buy from a dealer who will honor your warranty for life. A pack should last you twenty years, even when heavily used.

■ Make sure you fit the pack loaded with fifty pounds or so to get a realistic feel for how comfortable it will be on the trail. You should also make sure that your chest and belt straps are comfortable and allow sufficient tightening to distribute the load.

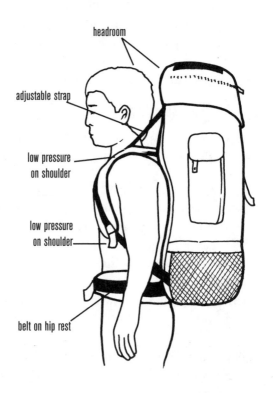

headroom

adjustable strap

low pressure
on shoulder

low pressure
on shoulder

belt on hip rest

Adjusting your pack

■ The weight of your backpack, surprisingly, can be a good portion of your gear weight, 10 to 15 percent. Extended-trip backpacks vary in weight from 4 to 8 pounds.

■ Get a pack with some outside pockets for storing day-use items.

■ Avoid built-in water bags. They are often difficult to fill with water or filter into. A good water bottle does not need fixing, is inexpensive to purchase or replace, and is easy to clean. Spend the money you could have spent on an expensive hydration system on a better tent or sleeping bag.

■ The best way to adjust your pack is to have it fitted properly when you buy it. Pick a dealer who will measure your torso length and correctly adjust a fully loaded pack in the store. The diagram on page 22 includes tips for a properly fitted pack.

■ A pack fly with hood that covers your head and back while hiking is really nice to have. Lots of pack flies cover your pack but don't cover the area between your pack and your back, where the water runs. In addition, hiking in full rain gear is often too hot, and a pack fly that extends out over your head allows you to make time without the on-and-off of rain gear.

Packing Your Pack

■ Ideally you should carry no more than one-third of your body weight. Carrying too much can cause permanent damage to your body. If you are hiking with a group, you should be able to distribute community items. If you are responsible for a group, you may end up with more weight. But if you are frugal, you may be able to get your pack down to around thirty pounds. You can always reduce weight even more by omitting items related to comfort—but do not cut weight by leaving your rain gear at home.

■ Use an inexpensive foam pad instead of heavier air mattresses (savings, 10 ounces).

■ Avoid heavy utility tools: A Swiss Army knife may be just as useful and lighter—plus you never know when you might have to open a bottle of fine wine (utility tool, 6 ounces; Swiss Army knife, 3.5 ounces). *NOTE:* Lighter utility tools do exist, but they often don't include some of the useful features of their full-size relatives.

■ Pay close attention to the weight of items that make up a large percentage of the total, like your tent (10 to 14 percent of gear weight), sleeping bag (9 to 11 percent), backpack (10 to 15 percent), and food (13 to 14 percent).

■ Use iodine tablets instead of a water filter to treat water, and carry some flavored drink mix to mask the taste (savings, 17.5 ounces).

■ Save space and weight by eating out of your cup

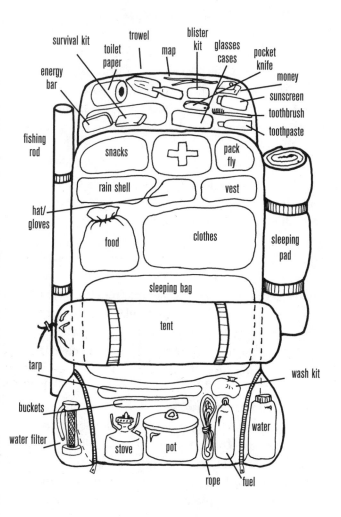

Packing your pack

and bringing only one pan (savings, 44 ounces).

■ On short trips in mild climates, carry food that does not need to be cooked, such as fruit, nuts, cheese, tortillas, granola, and crackers. Save weight and chores by leaving the stove and gas at home (savings, 63-plus ounces). —*Will Harmon*

■ Repackage food in plastic freezer or ziplock bags and reduce the amount of garbage, cardboard, and packaging you carry into the backcountry (savings, 10-plus ounces). —*Will Harmon*

■ Packing your backpack is often frustrating and time-consuming, but it is always important. Strive to balance the weight of your pack from side to side, and avoid sticking heavy objects like your tent on top or far away from your center of gravity. Pack items you might need during the day in an outside pocket or in the top of your pack.

■ Think of the order of your chores once you reach camp and what things you will actually use on the trail. At camp, chores may occur in the following order: Set up tent; throw in sleeping bag, pad, and clothes. At the food prep area, begin cooking dinner after gathering all food bags from group members. To make this process efficient, strap the tent and pad on the outside of your pack, and pack sleeping bag and clothes above cooking items. Items needed on the trail—such as rain gear, hat, gloves, fleece vest, snacks, sunglasses, sunscreen, bug dope, and first-aid kit—should either be in the top zippered portion of the pack, close to the top, or in an outside pocket.

■ Use mesh or nylon "ditty bags" to organize all small items into logical groups like personal kit and survival kit, and use them to split food into snacks, drinks, breakfast foods, and evening foods.

■ If you do not fill up your internal-frame pack, stuff the top portion of the pack into the main portion. This makes your pack smaller and distributes weight more evenly.

■ If you don't have a special clip in your backpack for attaching keys, use a safety pin to fasten your car key to the inside of your backpack so that you can be sure to have it when you get back to the trailhead.

■ For those who use external aluminum pack frames, throw in a few extra large paper clips. They can be used to replace the metal rings that sometimes come loose and disappear.

■ To repair a damaged backpack, waist belt, or shoulder strap, take a large sewing needle. Dental floss can double as heavy thread.

■ Carabiners clipped to loops on the outside of your pack can be very handy for clipping your boots on for a stream crossing and tying down exterior items. —*Fred Barstad*

Trailheads

■ Make sure you have good directions to the trailhead before heading out for your hike.

■ Before you leave for the trailhead, get as much information as you can about the area you are hiking. It doesn't hurt to get the most current information you can over the phone from the local managing agency (best from the people on the ground or at least someone at headquarters who keeps track of what the trail crew is doing). Web sites and guidebooks are good but can't keep up with every mudslide, trail closure, or ever-changing road conditions.

■ Check road conditions before leaving, and always inquire locally for current road conditions leading to the trailhead. Roads to backcountry trailheads are sometimes poorly maintained and are often winding dirt roads. Many trails start right from paved roads, especially in national parks, but others start from unpaved spur roads. Depending on road conditions and the remoteness of the trailhead, you may or may not need a high-clearance vehicle or four-wheel-drive capacity.

■ Save time by getting up early and driving to the trailhead before most tourists leave camp and clog the roads.

■ Roadside assistance service provided by insurance companies often ends when the pavement ends, giving new meaning to "off-road." Get a clear description of your coverage from your insurance company.

■ Do not expect the trailhead to be marked; trailhead signs are often victims of backcountry vandalism.

Foreign Trailheads

■ Backpacking abroad requires extensive research and preparation beyond any guidebook.

■ Be sure to start your passport and visa process at least six months in advance, and find out as much as you can from books, government resources, the Internet, and embassies before going abroad.

■ Avoid countries in the midst of political turmoil or war, and contact embassy officials in the country you intend to visit to inquire about any travel restrictions or warnings for potential visitors.

■ If you are planning to enter exotic rain forests or deserts, be sure to learn about dangerous plants and animals common to those areas.

■ For more information on obtaining a visa, contact:

Office of Visa Services
Bureau of Consular Affairs
U.S. Department of State
2201 C Street NW
Washington, DC 20520

■ If you are planning a trip outside North America, call the Centers for Disease Control (CDC) in Atlanta (404–332–4559) for up-to-date recommendations on vaccinations. *—Gilbert Preston, M.D.*

Vehicles and Keys

■ Place a hide-a-key somewhere on your vehicle in case you lose your keys, and make sure all members of the group know where it is.

■ Fasten your keys securely inside your pack.

■ Instead of exchanging keys midtrip, you can carry two sets of keys—one set for each group. If no exchange is made, you can start either car.

■ Unfortunately, trailhead crime is a concern, especially near urban areas. Lock your vehicle, and try not to leave anything valuable inside.

■ Deter trailhead theft by driving an old, beat-up car.

■ Arrange to be picked up so that you don't have to leave your vehicle at the trailhead.

■ Empty most of the contents of your wallet or purse before leaving home. Take only essentials: an all-purpose credit card, driver's license, fishing license, and emergency cash. This reduces the headache of replacement should the wallet become lost or soaked in a river. The same frugal policy goes for keys: Car and house keys should do the trick.
—*Rhonda and George Ostertag*

Weather

■ Probably the best way to predict the weather is to listen to the forecast and watch the general trend of weather. The exact timing of showers, snow, and sunshine often varies, but you can usually expect a forecasted change sometime within a two-day margin of error. High-altitude mountain ranges have their own weather, so be ready for anything, regardless of the forecast.

■ Watch cloud formations closely to avoid being caught at high altitude or on a ridgeline during a bad storm, especially when lightning is present.

■ Rain miles away can cause flash floods in canyons;

you should be especially cautious when hiking in slot canyons.

■ One of the pleasures of backpacking is the late-evening alpenglow, the reddish tint on the slopes of mountain peaks. So don't go to bed too early.

Lightning

■ Lightning can travel far, so be sure to take cover before the storm hits. Don't try to make it back to your vehicle; it isn't worth the risk. Instead seek shelter, even if it's only a short distance back to the trailhead. Lightning storms usually don't last long, and from a safe distance you might enjoy the sights and sounds.

■ Be especially careful not to be caught on an exposed ridge, near solitary trees, or near standing water. Seek shelter in low-lying areas—ideally a relatively dense stand of small-diameter trees such as lodgepole pines, common throughout the West.

■ Stay away from objects that might attract lightning, such as tent poles, graphite fishing poles, and metal food-hanging poles. Get in a crouched position, with both feet firmly on the ground or on your sleeping pad.

■ If you are caught in a bad place in a bad storm, spread your group apart at least 50 feet. If someone is struck, other members of the party will be available for first aid. Lightning victims have a good chance of revival with properly administered and maintained CPR.

■ Should you get out of your tent during a lightning storm? Generally, you should stay in your tent with your feet up on your sleeping pad. Exceptions include if you perched your tent on an exposed ridge. Some areas of the country have such severe lightning storms that they may warrant getting out of the tent and standing in the rain a short distance away in a stand of small trees. Much depends on your location, but rarely do we recommend setting up your tent atop a mountain or ridge, and rarely do we exit the tent during a lightning storm.

Dealing with Heat

■ The best way to deal with heat is to drink plenty of water. In a desert or dry, hot climate, wear light-colored clothing and cotton fabrics for hiking during the day. Carry extra water—and know where your next water source will be.

■ Preventing dehydration is safer than treating it. Drink a liter of water or sport drink an hour or two before you reach the trailhead. While hiking, drink a mouthful every twenty to thirty minutes.
—*Gilbert Preston, M.D.*

■ Always wear a hat, preferably one with a wide brim all around.

■ On hot days on familiar and good-quality trails, leave in the early morning (or before sunrise) and hike with a headlamp. Early rising allows you to take advantage of the cooler morning.
—*Rhonda and George Ostertag*

Dealing with Cold

■ The best way to deal with cold is to have the right clothes, drink lots of liquids, and bring extra fuel for cooking hot drinks.

■ Do not hike too fast; the sweat will make you cold. Slow down, and change wet clothing immediately.

■ Travel on snow or ice, even on cloudy days, requires 100 percent UV protection for eyes and a high-SPF sunscreen. —*Gilbert Preston, M.D.*

■ To protect against frostbite, allow enough room in boots and gloves to avoid blood vessel constriction. —*Gilbert Preston, M.D.*

Staying Found

■ Make sure you start at the right trailhead. If you have the opportunity to check with a ranger in the area before your trip, have him or her mark the correct trailhead on your map.

■ Periodically check your map as you travel, even if you are sure where you are. Note landmarks as you pass—the little ones. Make a mental note of a unique stump or an unmarked junction.

■ Trails that receive infrequent use often fade away in grassy meadows or on ridgetops. Fortunately, these sections are usually short. Make a mental note of your last location where you knew you really were on the trail. Come back to that point as you foray outward in a circle to find the continuance of the trail. Don't rule out a sharp turn or that you missed a turn 100 yards back and what you thought was the trail was actually a game trail.

■ As you hike, look for signs of human disturbance to indicate that you are on the right route or at least a maintained trail. Make a mental note of cairns (human-constructed piles of rocks), chainsaw-cut logs, trail markers, trail crew, drainage work, etc.

■ If you get lost, don't panic. Sit down and relax. Look at your map. Take a map, compass, or, better yet, GPS reading. Next, develop a probable location mind-set and retrace your steps back to your last point of location confidence. Then move forward to your trip destination.

■ If you can't find the last known place of confidence, you are lost, at least temporarily. Again, it is worth the time to sit for a while with your map and navigation tools—or even take a break from them. You need to clear your head enough to think logically. Rambling aimlessly most often leads you in circles or to a greater degree of loss.

■ Many people get lost in the wilderness and survive. Your chance of harm is still far less than your chance of injury in a car accident on your morning commute.

■ For safety, always carry a topographic map. The key on the map should tell you the scale. For 7.5-minute quadrangles, the scale is 1:24,000, which means that 1 inch on the map is equivalent to 24,000 inches (2,000 feet) on the ground. Contour intervals give the elevation gain or loss when crossing each line. The most common contour interval is 40 feet, but you may also have maps with 100-, 80-, 50-, or 20-foot intervals. Widely spaced contour lines indicate less elevation change; closely spaced lines indicate steep terrain. Lines directly on top of each other indicate cliffs.

■ Do not wait until you are confused to look at your maps. When you start up the trail, begin monitoring your location so that you have a continual fix on your location.

■ To keep from getting lost, orient yourself to natural "handrails"—mountain ridges, valleys, streams, and shorelines—that follow your general line of travel. —*Will Harmon*

■ When you've the lost trail, do not underestimate the quality of a game trail and mistake it for a human trail—especially in areas with free-range cattle or bison or even high-quality elk habitat. Animal routes are heavily used and easy to follow, but they do not necessarily lead anywhere. Look for those trail signs that only humans can make.

■ Do not trust blazes or flagging; treat them as a topographic clue, not a rule. Who knows why a person would flag a certain spot—could be he or she got lost just like you. Blazes become grown over with bark over time. Do not sit there staring at the blaze, wondering if it was made by an ax; use your map, compass, and GPS instead. Even if it was made by an ax, you don't know why this particular tree was blazed or in what decade.

■ Remember your last-known confident point.

Finding Your Location with a Compass

■ A compass has an arrow mounted on a baseplate that points to magnetic north. Magnetic north is not real north, but you can adjust for real north by drawing a line extending from and in the direction of the magnetic-north arrow (MN) located on the bottom of your map. Align the compass along this line and turn the map gently until the magnetic arrow lines up with north on the compass.

■ Use the direction-of-travel arrow on the baseplate or a slotted sighting device to take bearings of two or three landmarks around you. Aim the direction-of-travel arrow at a known landmark, hold the compass steady and level, rotate the dial so that the 0 or magnetic north is lined up exactly with the floating arrow. The corresponding number at the direction-of-travel arrow is the bearing of the landmark. Draw a line on your map on the known landmark in the direction of the bearing (degree).

■ For example, you are hiking around Mount Defiance and you lose the trail. Fortunately, through breaks in the clouds you see Bear Lake and the radio tower on top of the mountain. (See illustration on page 39.)

■ Take a bearing for Bear Lake and Mount Defiance, and draw lines on the map. (See illustration on page 41.)

■ If drawn to "known" landmarks at different bearings, the intersection of two lines is your location. For three lines, you are in the triangle, hence the name triangulation. In the illustration, the two lines cross at a point below the trail on the map, and the

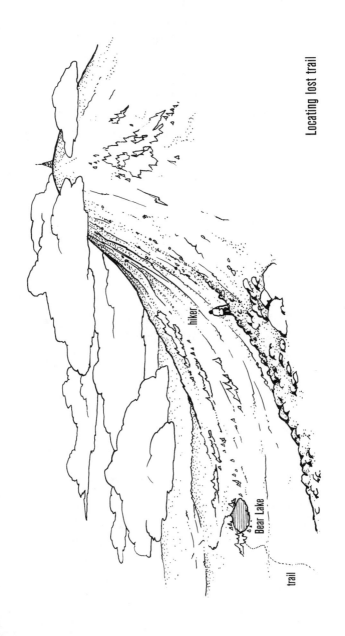

Locating lost trail

Bear Lake

trail

hiker

trail itself is probably just a short walk uphill. Unfortunately, you do not always have "known" landmarks. If you anticipate hiking off-trail, learn to use a global positioning system (GPS) and start from a known point. Thick forest and other natural features may interfere with readings, but even an occasional reading is helpful.

Using GPS

■ A global positioning system (GPS) receiver is a navigation device that allows you to locate your position via satellite communication. GPS will not help you if you do not have and know how to read a topographic map.

■ GPS is especially useful for expeditions where your exact location may be a life-or-death matter and for trail hikes and canoe trips in areas with little elevation change or visible landmarks.

■ Learning to use GPS takes practice—and is a book in itself.

■ Be sure to take extra batteries for your GPS.

■ If you use a GPS receiver to help with backcountry navigation, buy maps preprinted with the metric Universal Transverse Mercator (UTM) grid, or draw

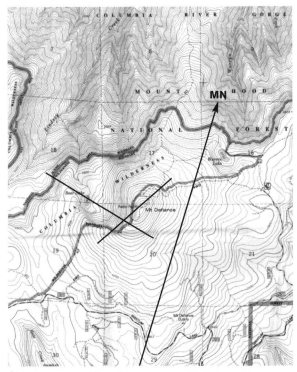

Two lines, drawn on map with degree measurements

the gridlines yourself before the trip. UTM is much easier to use in the field than latitude and longitude.
—*Bruce Grubbs*

■ For more information on the basics of GPS navigation, the authors recommend *Basic Essentials Using GPS* by Bruce Grubbs.

■ If your GPS shows your location as different from where you think you are, and you have triple-checked your reading and map-marking work, *trust* the GPS receiver.

If You Get Lost

■ If you get lost, do not panic. Sit down and relax for a few minutes while you carefully check your topographic map and take a reading with your compass.

■ Do not run. Panic will only make you more disoriented, and running will take you farther from your last point of known location.

■ Confidently plan your next move. It is always smart to retrace your steps until you find familiar ground, even if you think it might lengthen your trip. Many people (even experienced hikers) get temporarily lost in the wilderness but survive by calmly and rationally dealing with the situation.

■ If you decide to stay put, signal for help. In an open area, build a smoky fire, blow your whistle three times, and yell at the top of your lungs, but do not waste energy by yelling too much. Spread anything unnaturally colored across the ground or build an "SOS" to alert air rescue. Do what you can, and keep calm. Most people are rescued within three days.

Sharing

■ Hikers do not have the trails to themselves. Be the first to yield to others and give a friendly hello. If you meet a horse party on the trail, move off the trail on the downhill side and quietly let the animals pass. It is too difficult (and sometimes dangerous) for horses to yield. Mountain bikers should yield to hikers, but it is often safer for the hiker to step off the trail and let a mountain biker pass.

Pacing Yourself

■ Do not exhaust yourself by traveling too far or too fast. Walk as naturally as possible whether going up or downhill. If you get tired, slow down.

■ When laboring up a big hill with a big pack, loosen the chest strap. It allows you to breathe more easily when you need all the breath you can get.

■ Sing quietly as you walk the trail, especially when hiking alone. If you cannot sing without being out of breath, you are overdoing it. Also, be careful not to run off your hiking companions.
—*Donna Ikenberry*

■ If you have knee problems, consider using light-weight hiking poles. —*Donna Ikenberry*

Group Travel

■ Do not hike alone. Every safety and outdoor

expert tells you this—but then they take the afternoon off to go hiking by themselves. We both hike solo occasionally, but it's clearly safer to travel in groups. If someone is injured, there is someone to go for help. If there are only two hikers, the victim must be stable to allow the other to go for help; otherwise, he or she must stay and care for the victim and wait for help. Thus, two people are only a little better than one person; groups of at least three and preferably four hikers are much safer.

■ Don't exhaust your party by traveling too far or too fast. Let the slowest person set the pace.

■ When you do have a party of three or more, stay together so that you don't lose the safety benefits of a group.

■ The easiest way to keep your group together is to have the slowest person hike first and everyone else follow. This works well as long as the abilities of the group are similar. More practically, this strategy is fine on the flats and downhills, but on the climbs it is just too hard to walk behind someone vastly slower than you are, especially with a heavy backpack. Always regroup near the top of the climb or a predetermined meeting place. If you are feeling spry, you can always walk back down to the slower member of your party and summit with them again.

■ Always regroup at trail junctions. This avoids the worry of "did they take the wrong fork." Who knows? You may want to consult with the rest of your party if you don't know the "right fork" in the trail.

■ Groups should stay together or split into two smaller groups if you have enough people, with each group having a designated leader (or natural one). When people get separated on climbs, faster hikers should wait for slower hikers as soon as they get out of sight of one another.

■ There is nothing worse than fearing the worst, when all that has happened is a little miscommunication. Save yourself a lot of stress and increase your level of safety by staying together.

Going Solo

■ Definitely leave your itinerary with a friend or relative—where you are going, when you will be back, and how long to wait before alerting the authorities.

■ Do not take chances alone that you might take with a group.

■ Bring your survival kit.

■ Make extra noise in bear country, and watch for stalking mountain lions in lion country.

■ Bring and use your watch. Be realistic about how much time it will take you to get back to where you said you would be at the time you said you would be there.

Fording Rivers

■ Research your hike in advance to make sure it does not involve a ford.

■ Crossing a river can be safe, but you must know your limits. Sometimes you simply should turn back. Even if only one member of your party (such as a child) might not be able to follow larger, stronger members, you should not try a risky ford. Be confident. If you are not a strong swimmer, learn to be. Strong swimming skills give you confidence.

■ Just like with getting lost, panic at a ford can easily make the situation worse. Another way to build confidence is to practice. Find a small stream and carefully practice crossing it both with a pack and without one.

■ When you get to a ford, don't automatically cross at the point where the trail comes to the stream. A river can reform each spring during runoff, so a ford that was safe last year might be too deep this year. Study upstream and downstream sections, and look for a place where the stream widens and the water is not more than waist deep on the shortest member of your party.

■ Crossing a stream above a logjam can be extremely dangerous. The water flowing beneath the logs may "dive" as it approaches them. The strong current can easily suck the unwary hiker under water beneath the logs, from where there may be no escape. —*Fred Barstad*

■ When faced with the choice of crossing on a wet log or fording a stream, wading is the safer choice. —*Ron Adkison*

■ Carry a stabilizing stick that can also double as a prod for extricating yourself from mud or silt. —*Bert and Jane Gildart*

■ Crossing rivers step by step:
1. Make sure your matches, camera, billfold, clothes, sleeping bag, and any other items you must keep dry are in watertight bags.

2. Have dry clothes ready when you get to the other side of the river to minimize the risk of hypothermia.

3. Do not try a ford with bare feet. Wear hiking boots without socks, sneakers, or tightly strapped sandals.

4. Undo the belt straps on your pack. If you fall in

and are washed downstream, a waterlogged pack can anchor you to the bottom. You must be able to get out of your pack easily.

5. Minimize your time in the water, but do not rush; go slowly and deliberately.

6. Take one step at a time. Make sure each foot is securely planted before lifting the other foot. Avoid large, slick rocks in favor of gravel beds.

7. Take a 45-degree downstream angle, and follow a riffle line if possible.

8. Stay sideways with the current—turning upstream or downstream increases the force of the current against you. In some cases, two or three people can cross together, locking forearms with the strongest person on the upstream side.

■ If you have a choice, ford in the early morning, when the stream is not as deep. In the mountains the cool evening temperatures slow snowmelt and reduce the water flow into the rivers. On small streams, a sturdy walking stick used on the upstream side for balance can help prevent a fall, but in a major river with a fast current, a walking stick offers little help.

■ If you have to swim, do not panic. Do not try to swim directly across. Instead, pick a long angle and gradually cross to the other side, taking as much as

100 yards or more to get across. If your pack starts to drag you down, get out of it immediately, even if you have to abandon it. If you lose control and are washed downstream, go feet first so that you do not hit your head on rocks or logs.

Dealing with Downfall

■ In burn areas or areas where wet soil and high winds can combine to bring down trees, it is impossible for trail crews to clear every downed tree immediately. So expect to be climbing over a few logs on many trails in the backcountry. In most cases, it is safer to go over logs slowly, without actually stepping on the log. Downfall is often unstable, and putting your weight on it could make it roll or bounce, a sure way to twist an ankle—or worse. Also, bark can slip off the log unexpectedly and cause you to take a nasty fall.

■ To save energy when hiking, step over logs rather than stepping up onto a log, and then down. Not only will you expend less energy, but in the course of a day, you will take fewer total steps.
—*Bert and Jane Gildart*

■ The only sane way to travel through thick downfall, especially winter lodgepole pine forests, is via state of mind. Peaceful enjoyment of the moment slows you down, keeps the journey safe, and makes it a fun and challenging situation. —*Bill Hunger*

Bugs

■ The blackflies of Maine, the fire ants in Texas, the mosquitoes of Yellowstone, or bugs anywhere can make your trip miserable, so be prepared.

■ In northern-tier states, August or September frosts often kill off most bugs.

■ The most common way to deal with biting insects is repellent, usually one containing DEET. Although we know that DEET can be harmful, we use it because it is the only thing that really works. Citronella is at best only partially effective. A compromise is to concentrate a DEET application on your clothes, socks, and hat. Avoid direct application to the skin until you just can't take the bugs another minute. Putting DEET on clothing does not work for "fashion" hikers, because DEET eats through plastic and discolors clothing (even more reason not to put it on your skin).

■ DEET may also help prevent painful but mostly harmless wasp, hornet, yellow jacket, and bee stings. If you are allergic to bee stings, consult your doctor before going outdoors, and be sure to include an anaphylaxis emergency kit with your personal first-aid kit.

■ Bug nets are light and cheap and can be a lifesaver. You can get nets to fit over your hat and face to keep bugs at bay while you're hiking; you also can put bug nets over your face while sleeping.

■ You can put on your rain gear to prevent bites and stings, but be sure to drink enough liquids to avoid dehydration once you are all bundled up.

■ Tuck a bandana into the back brim of a cap to protect the nape of your neck from biting flies and mosquitoes. —*Will Harmon*

■ Where bugs are abundant, make camp near ridgetops or open slopes where breezes will help hold bugs at bay. —*Will Harmon*

Ticks, Snakes, and Scorpions, Oh My!

■ Tick season is usually April through June. Unlike other biting insects, ticks do not bite right away; they crawl around and find a nice, warm, hairy spot and dig in. You can prevent bites by wearing long pants and checking your body regularly for ticks, including your head and pubic and rectal areas.

■ Tiny deer ticks can cause Lyme disease. Larger ticks can carry Rocky Mountain spotted fever. If you experience flulike symptoms and/or a spotted or measleslike rash, see a doctor immediately. Both conditions are treatable but can be fatal if not treated properly.

■ When hiking in tick-infested areas, it is a good idea to wear light-colored pants with drawstrings around the ankles, but many of us find shorts to be more comfortable on warm days. If you wear shorts, look at and rub your hands over your bare legs often (every few minutes). You will catch most of the critters this way; they usually land and crawl on your body below the knees. —*Fred Barstad*

■ You can close your pants around your ankles with duct tape to prevent tick entry.

■ Although there are many methods for removing ticks, it is best to use forceps or tweezers, grasp the tick closely around its entire body, and pull straight out, gently and firmly. Afterward scrub and sterilize the area. If you're worried about Lyme disease or Rocky Mountain spotted fever, keep the tick in a zip-lock bag and have it tested when you return home.

■ In snake country carry a snakebite kit in your first-aid kit. Neither snakes nor scorpions are aggressive; they only bite or sting in self-defense. When traveling in snake country, do not reach under rocks or into crevices, which are common places for snakes to hide from the hot sun. If you hike or camp in areas known to support poisonous snakes or scorpions, be cautious and check sleeping bags, boots, and backpacks carefully for uninvited guests.

■ Sleep in a tent with your screen zipped up and you will not wake up with unexpected visitors.

■ Be careful lighting fires. They often drive scorpions from rocks and wood.

■ If you see a snake or scorpion, stay clear. If you are bitten, stay calm, clean, and disinfect the area, and seek medical attention. Many people survive snake and scorpion bites without treatment, but you should consult a physician to increase your survival rate to 100 percent.

■ In areas inhabited by scorpions, always shake out your boots and clothing before putting them on in the morning. —*Ron Adkison*

Wildlife Watching

■ Stay clear of all wild animals. If your viewing an animal changes its natural behavior, you are too close. Disturbing wildlife endangers both wildlife and future wildlife watching. Large hoofed animals can charge when they feel threatened.

■ Do not feed animals. Feeding by humans can make animals dependent on human food, which lacks the nutrients animals need to build up sufficient fat stores for the winter. Often this means starvation for fed animals—a fed animal is a dead animal.

■ Bison look tame, slow, and docile, but the opposite is true in all cases. Always give bison a wide berth.

Water and Water Filters

■ All hikers should take steps to make sure the water they drink is pure. The best way is to boil water rapidly for ten minutes and add a droplet of bleach, letting it stand for twenty minutes thereafter. However, this is not always convenient, and water filters have come a long way, killing at the very least *Giardia*. Follow local recommendations for treating water, and always carry backup means. We personally carry backup iodine tablets, filter drinking water, and boil dinner water.

■ Before you leave on a trip, check the distances between water sources. If you have long stretches without access to water, carry extra.

■ Because of waterborne microorganisms that can make you sick, even clear mountain water is not safe to drink. Treating or filtering water is a necessity.

■ We prefer regular water bottles to new hydration systems. The benefit of drinking more water along the trail is outweighed by the inconvenience of filtering water repeatedly into plastic pouches.

■ Buy a water filter that you can repair and maintain. Carry replacement parts for your filter, and know how to fix it.

■ Lubricate filter parts according to the manufacturer's recommendations. It will pump water faster, be easier to take apart, and produce purer water.

■ After filtering, make sure you empty all the water left in the filter. You can do this quickly on some filters by unscrewing the top and pouring out excess water. If this is not a convenient option, make sure to really pump the filter dry.

■ Filters vary widely in reliability and effectiveness. Buy a model that allows for field cleaning and repair, and check consumer reviews.

■ As an alternative to filters, go with iodine tablets and lemon flavor to cover up the taste. It's much lighter than carrying a filter.

■ If you have intense diarrhea or vomiting within several weeks of a backpacking trip, see a doctor immediately. Giardiasis and other waterborne illnesses can be life threatening.

■ Carry a plastic coffee-filter holder and a few paper coffee filters to screen water before treating it with iodine or a filter. This removes debris before treatment. —*Bruce Grubbs*

■ When drawing water from a silty stream, allow water to settle in a collapsible bucket or pan; this will extend the life of your filter. —*Ron Adkison*

■ In desert canyons, if you expect flooding, treat ample water before flooding. Muddy floodwaters can remain too turbid to use for eight to twenty-four hours. —*Ron Adkison*

■ Since water filters break down, always carry a backup means of water purification, such as iodine tablets. —*Ron Adkison*

Tent Sites

■ Find a durable surface, at least 100 feet from water and on flat ground. Be wary of bowl-shaped areas and careful of depressions. Do not dig trenches. Instead, pick a spot that will stay dry even under heavy rains.

■ In bear country, make sure your tent site is at least 100 yards away from your food preparation area and food-hanging pole.

■ Using a space blanket as a ground cloth can keep your tent warm. On cool nights put the silver reflective side up and set up your tent on it. On warm nights put the red nonreflective side up for a cooler floor.

■ If you have to set your tent up in the rain, first spread it out, and then immediately put your fly over it. Then push the poles through while keeping the tent under the fly. You can also set up a tarp and then set up the tent under the tarp.

■ When setting up camp under tall trees, look up for "widowmakers," large dead branches and trees that could come crashing down. Widowmakers are especially common in mature ponderosa pine forests. —*Bruce Grubbs*

■ When backpacking in desert canyons, always camp above the high water-mark, indicated by a line of debris on benches and canyon walls, to avoid the potentially fatal results of flash floods. —*Ron Adkison*

Designated Campsites

■ Most national parks and some national forests require backpackers to stay in designated campsites. If so, try to reserve your campsite in advance to save you from having to stand in line at a visitor center once you get there. Before trying to reserve a campsite, however, make sure you have checked the restrictions. Many campsites do not allow campfires, and you won't be able to reserve sites that are closed due to the season and protection of fragile wildlife resources.

■ Do not assume that all campsites are easy to find or have a noticeable trailside sign. Vandals knock down and steal signs. Keep the map out. When you get close to the campsite, watch carefully for it so that you do not have to backtrack.

■ Ask the ranger giving you the permit for specific directions to the campsite, and mark the exact location on your topographic map.

Sleeping under the Stars

■ We have both slept outside the tent in dry weather, but not in areas supporting snakes, scorpions, and bears. You also may weigh the consequences of a wet sleeping bag. If you are sure it is not going to rain, you are not worried about creatures of the night, and you have a warm enough bag, find a soft spot and enjoy a night under the stars.

■ When you sleep out, use a lightweight bag cover or bivy sac. It will add 10 degrees Fahrenheit of warmth to your sleeping bag, even more if it is breezy. —*Bruce Grubbs*

■ A small draping of mosquito netting that covers the face held up by three or four sticks placed upright in the ground around the head can make outside sleeping and stargazing a summertime possibility. —*Bill Hunger*

Campfires

■ Regulations prohibit campfires in some parts of the backcountry, but if you are in an area where

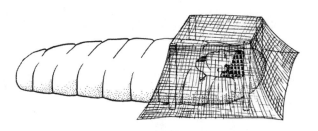

Mosquito net over head for sleeping under the stars

fires are allowed, treat yourself. Besides adding to nightly entertainment, the fire might make your camp safer from bears because you can burn all food scraps and garbage to eliminate food smell.

■ Avoid building campfires in pristine areas, especially where downed wood is in short supply. Evidence of past campfires invites others to build a fire of their own. —*Ron Adkison*

■ Using an already established fire ring minimizes impact in an area. Moreover, if it is a popular camping spot, leaving that ring clean encourages the next camper to use it. —*Bill Hunger*

■ Make your own lightweight fire pan by cutting a 2-foot square of flame-retardant canvas from an old discarded wall tent. —*Will Harmon*

■ For an emergency or wet-weather fire starter, carry a single briquette of match-light charcoal

wrapped in foil and sealed in a plastic ziplock bag.
—*Will Harmon*

■ Never plan to use a fire for cooking. If you need warm liquids, use your stove.

■ When you cannot find dry wood, look at the base of a spruce.

■ Building a fire for an emergency is very different from building one on a warm, dry night to roast marshmallows. Wet snow can make it hard to find dry wood. Don't break off branches unless it is an emergency. Emergencies take precedence over zero-impact concerns.

■ Almost everyone develops his or her own way of starting a campfire, but two of the most common methods are the Log Cabin and Tepee Styles. The names are structurally descriptive: You build a log cabin for the first and a tepee for the second, and then you start your fire in the middle. Below are the basics for building an emergency fire and a zero-impact fire.

■ Building an emergency/survival fire:
  1. Gather all the materials you need to start your fire.
  2. Cover your wood with a garbage bag or tarp.

Log Cabin Fire

Tepee Fire

3. Build a small log cabin with 0.25- to 0.5-inch-diameter pieces.

4. Take some toilet paper or a paper towel and put it in the middle of the log cabin. Light the paper and feed it with the smallest of dry twigs until it starts to burn the log cabin. If you do not have any small-diameter twigs, use your knife to shave some dry chips. If you are having trouble making the fire go, take a wad of toilet paper and soak it in gas or smear fire paste on it before lighting it in the center of your log cabin.

5. Once the fire is burning, feed it rapidly, especially if it is raining. Once you have the fire burning, you can pile logs loosely on top. The smoke will dry them out so that they will burn and you can repeat the drying and burning process.

6. Be careful to allow space and air in the log

cabin. Do not smother it with too much wood at a time, and blow gently to feed the flame.

7. If you don't have paper to light your fire, cut a ball of pitch or sap from a nearby tree. Sap will burn for several minutes once lit.

■ Building a zero-impact fire:

1. Gather small-diameter, dead, down wood.

2. With a trowel, dig a 12-inch-diameter pit through organic layers, then set the soil aside with the top layer intact.

3. Put kindling and paper in the hole and light the fire.

4. Burn only small pieces, less than an inch thick, down to fine white ash.

5. Soak the ashes with water.

6. Replace the soil and make the area look as though there was no fire.

■ Before leaving camp the next morning, dig out the fire pit or check the area where you had a fire. Make sure it is cold to the touch and completely out before leaving. Pack out any scorched foil and cans left by other campers.

Cooking

■ Be careful not to spill on yourself while cooking. If you do, change clothes and hang the clothes with food odor with the food and garbage. Wash your hands thoroughly before retiring to the tent.

■ Do not cook too much food so that you do not have to deal with leftovers. If you do end up with extra food, carry it out. Don't bury it, throw it in a lake, or leave it. Animals will find and dig up any food or garbage buried in the ground.

■ If you can have a campfire and decide to cook fish, try cooking them in aluminum-foil envelopes instead of frying them. After removing the cooked fish, quickly and completely burn the fish scraps off the foil. Using foil also means you do not have to wash the pan you used to cook the fish.

■ Never cook in your tent; you could easily die from carbon monoxide poisoning. Plus, in bear country you do not want food smell in your tent.

■ Carry all garbage out.

■ Prepare for garbage problems before you leave home. Carry in as little potential garbage as possible by discarding excess packaging while packing. Bring along airtight ziplock bags to store garbage. Be sure to hang your garbage at night along with your food.

Washing Dishes

■ Washing dishes is a sticky problem, but there is one easy solution: If you don't dirty dishes, you don't have to wash them. Try to minimize food smell by using as few dishes and pans as possible.

■ Remove food scraps from pans and dishes with paper towels before washing them. When you wash dishes, you'll have much less food smell.

■ Burn the dirty towels, or store them in ziplock bags with other garbage.

■ Put pans and dishes in ziplock bags before putting them back in your pack.

■ If you end up with lots of food scraps in the dishwater, strain out the scraps and store them in ziplock bags with other garbage.

■ Do dishes immediately after eating so that a minimum of food smell lingers in the area.

■ Never wash dishes in a stream or lake, and use as little biodegradable soap as possible.

■ Bring a lightweight screen to filter out food scraps from dishwater, but be sure to store the screen with the food and garbage.

■ If you have a campfire, pour the dishwater around the edge of the fire. If you don't have a fire or if pouring dishwater on the rocks of the fire is prohibited, take the dishwater at least 100 yards downwind and downhill from camp and pour it on the ground. Do not put dishwater or food scraps in a lake or stream.

■ Cut a small strip of material from a quick-dry towel. Use it for washing your pots or bowls, then wring it out and use it for drying them.
—*Donna Ikenberry*

Storing and Hanging Food

■ Be sure to check local regulations for storing food. Some areas require bear-proof containers or other secure storage methods, and hanging food may be discouraged or illegal in these areas. This is especially true in California national parks where black bears have long since figured out how to take down a food bag hung in a tree.

■ It is best to hang your food. To be as safe as possible, store everything that has any food smell away from your sleeping area. This includes cooking gear, eating utensils, food bags, garbage—even clothes with food smells on them.

■ If the campsite doesn't have a pole or food-storage container, be sure to set one up or at least locate one before it gets dark. It is not only difficult and potentially dangerous to store food after dark, but it also is easier to miss a morsel on the ground.

■ Hang food in airtight, waterproof bags to prevent food odors from circulating throughout the forest. For double protection, put food and garbage in zip-lock bags and then seal them tightly in a larger plastic bag.

■ The illustrations on pages 66 and 67 depict three popular methods for hanging food. In any case, try to get food and garbage at least 10 feet off the ground and 4 feet from any tree.

■ Test the stability of the branch by pulling on both ends of the strung rope, but do not do this while standing directly under the branch.

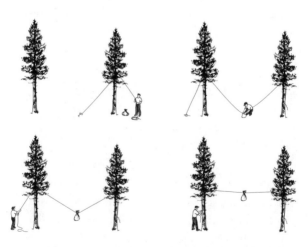

Hanging food and garbage between two trees

Hanging food and garbage over a tree branch

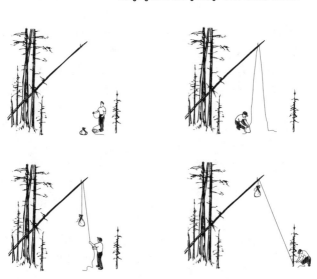

Hanging food and garbage over a leaning tree

■ Tie a good knot, wrap the rope around the tree several times, and tie a safety knot. Food coming down during the night can cause animal conflicts and could hurt another party using the same food pole.

■ You do not need a heavy climbing rope to store food. Go light instead. Parachute cord will usually suffice unless you plan to hang large quantities of food and gear (which might be the case on a long backpacking excursion or with a large group).

■ You can buy a small pulley or use a couple of carabiners to make hoisting a heavy load easier.

■ The classic method for getting the rope up over a branch or pole is by tying a rock or piece of wood to the end of your rope and tossing it over. Try to use something other than a rock, which can easily swing back and hit you in the head. If you carry a carabiner, you can attach the end of your rope to a small stuff sack with a little weight in it. Throw it over and unclip the bag and clip on your food bag. Use gloves so that you don't get rope burns. Don't let anybody stand under the bag until you are sure it is securely in place.

■ Once you have untied your food, slowly pull your rope over the branch. Do not jerk it. If the rope is stuck, you may have to leave it behind, unless you can duct tape a knife to a long branch and cut the rope. (With this retrieval method, you can often score some extra parachute cord left by others.)

■ Smaller rodents and flying squirrels can also be a problem. Many heavily used areas have food-storage areas; take advantage of these if their use is required and if they appear to work. If the managing agency has provided a food-storage device, use it instead of hanging food.

■ Aggressive birds and rodents can peck through your tent, another good reason to store food in an animal-proof container or hang your food, depending upon local regulations.

The Wilderness Restroom

■ Many uncomfortable conversations in the backcountry surround the basic function of going to the bathroom. There is no bathroom at most backcountry sites, but in heavy-use areas, use existing facilities. When you do not have a toilet, urinate at least 200 feet from water.

■ For getting rid of solid human waste, here are the basics:

1. Find a secluded spot at least 200 feet from water.

2. Dig a hole at least 6 inches deep.

3. Drop your drawers.

4. Squat down, using an arm for support or a log if you picked a good spot.

5. Relax and do your business.

6. Fill the hole with the dirt and sod; try to make it look as though there was never a hole.

■ For alpine ascents or heavily used areas, consider using a "poop tube" (a 4-inch-diameter piece of PVC pipe capped at one end and threaded for a screw-on lid on the other end) and pack out all solid waste.

■ Be sure to check local regulations for restrictions on the disposal of human waste. To avoid more restrictive regulations, be extra careful with waste.

■ Buried tampons or pads may attract—and be dug up by—wild animals. There might be pit toilets in the backcountry where disposal is allowed, but in most cases plan on packing such items out with the rest of your garbage.

■ Store used feminine hygiene products in a double-bagged, ziplock bag. Use sanitary wipes for cleaning hands. Pack these out with used tampons and pads.

Medical Emergencies

■ Wilderness first aid is a book in itself. In most cases you cannot call 911 until you get back to the trailhead or town. Even then, an ambulance cannot always drive right to you, and rural areas often have limited medical facilities. A sensible minimum precaution is to take a course on first aid and CPR. Neither this book nor any other book can teach you how to react to all emergencies, but a few guidelines are offered.

■ Carry a first-aid kit that includes at least the following items: sewing needle, snakebite kit, antiseptic swabs, butterfly bandages, adhesive strips, aspirin, antiseptic gel, gauze pads, triangular bandage, splints, moleskin, Second Skin, and gauze rolls.

■ For your first-aid kit, you can use scissors from your pocketknife or buy a "Micro" Leatherman and designate it to your first-aid kit. Some people like to have heavy-duty first-aid scissors to cut away clothing without having to move the victim's leg.

■ A conscious victim must grant permission before you can administer first aid.

■ Diabetics should carry all needed sugar and insulin supplies and be sure that other members of their party know where the supplies are and what signs to look for when they are needed.

■ If you encounter an accident victim on the trail, first calm down; then evaluate the scene and check

the ABCs: airway, breathing, and circulation.
—*Gilbert Preston, M.D.*

■ To be really well prepared for backcountry accidents, take a Wilderness First Responder Course.
—*Gilbert Preston, M.D.*

■ To treat insulin shock, the diabetic and all members of the group should carry an instant form of glucose, such as packets of sugar or a package of cake frosting. —*Gilbert Preston, M.D.*

■ Study first aid before you leave home; know what you are doing before you need to do it.

■ Don't eat wild plants unless you have positively identified them and know they are safe to eat. Also, make sure local public land regulations do not prohibit the consumption of certain wild plants for environmental/habitat reasons.

Altitude

■ Above 8,000 feet, altitude can cause problems for any outdoor adventure. Altitude sickness can be life threatening, but it has a simple cure—get to a lower altitude. If you or a companion experiences headaches, loss of appetite, loss of energy, nausea, difficulty sleeping, and/or low urine output, descend 2,000 to 4,000 feet as soon as possible. Help anyone who cannot get to a lower altitude alone, and never leave someone who exhibits symptoms of altitude illness.

■ Drink lots of water.

■ Be advised that above 10,000 feet elevation the oxygen amount in the air diminishes, and one's pace must often be slowed to accommodate that fact.
—*Bill Hunger*

■ Carry throat lozenges on high-altitude trips for a sore, raspy throat caused by dry air and increased rate of breathing. —*Gilbert Preston, M.D.*

Hypothermia

■ Be aware of the danger of hypothermia, a condition in which the internal temperature of the body drops below normal. It can lead to mental and physical collapse and death. With full-blown hypothermia, as energy reserves are exhausted cold reaches the brain, depriving you of good judgment and reasoning power. You won't be aware that this is happening. You lose control of your hands. Your internal temperature slides downward. Without treatment, this slide leads to stupor, collapse, and death.

■ If your party is exposed to wind, cold, and wet, think hypothermia. Watch yourself and others for these symptoms: uncontrollable fits of shivering; vague, slow, slurred speech; memory lapses; incoherence; immobile or fumbling hands; frequent stumbling or a lurching gait; drowsiness (to sleep is to die); apparent exhaustion; and inability to get up after a rest. When a member of your party has hypothermia, he or she may deny any problem. Believe the symptoms, not the victim.

■ To defend yourself against hypothermia, stay dry. Wet clothes lose about 90 percent of their insulating value. Wool loses relatively less heat. Cotton, down, and some synthetics lose more. Choose rain clothes that cover the head, neck, body, and legs and provide good protection against wind-driven rain. Most hypothermia cases develop in air temperatures between 30 and 50 degrees Fahrenheit, but hypothermia can develop in warmer temperatures. Dress in layers, drink lots of water, and eat foods high in carbohydrates and fats while engaged in strenuous outdoor exercise.

■ Set up camp early to avoid exposure to nighttime temperatures.

■ Exposure to cold, moisture, wind, dehydration, and exhaustion can all cause hypothermia. The moment you begin to lose heat faster than your body produces it, you're suffering from exposure. Your body starts involuntary exercise, such as shivering, to stay warm and makes involuntary adjustments to preserve normal temperature in vital organs, restricting blood flow to the extremities. Both responses drain your energy reserves. The only way to stop the drain is to reduce the degree of exposure.

■ For mild but possibly wet-weather camping, fleece sleeping bag liners greatly increase the temperature range of a synthetic sleeping bag.
—*Fred Barstad*

■ If you get cold, warm up before you get colder. Remove wet clothing. Keep moving. Eat something. Move your arms in circles to get blood to your fingertips. If you have to, set up your tent and get into your sleeping bag. —*Donna Ikenberry*

■ Watch for symptoms of hypothermia: uncontrollable fits of shivering, slowed speech, memory lapses, drowsiness, apparent exhaustion, or fumbling hands. An obvious sign is a person struggling to put his or her gloves back on, shivering in the process.

■ When you suspect hypothermia, get the victim out of wet clothes and into a dry sleeping bag. If the victim is only mildly affected, administer warm drinks. If the person is badly impaired, never give anything to drink, and watch for shock. If the victim's condition is deteriorating or if the symptoms are severe, have another person get into the sleeping bag skin to skin to transfer heat. Or double-bag, with two people on either side of the victim. Water heated and poured into heat-resistant Nalgene bottles can be placed in the sleeping bag between the victim's armpits and legs. Be sure to wrap the hot bottles in wool socks or other material so that you don't burn the victim.

When to Bail

■ Should I stay or should I go back? For recreational backpacking trips, you should bail on the trip if continuing creates a more life-threatening situation. Obviously, staying in your car could be safer (although statistics suggest that the drive to the trailhead is much more dangerous than any extended backcountry trip), but if you are ill prepared, heading into bad or worsening weather, or just not having a good time, there is no shame in going home early. Being safe and sound and having a hot meal and a hotel room is better than having to be rescued by a helicopter.

Desert Backpacking

■ Backpacking in the desert is, simply put, more exercise and more limited by physical strength and stamina. You really can't avoid the weight, because you need to carry water.

■ Experts recommend packing one gallon of water per person per day. For many people, this essentially limits the length of your trip to two or three nights.

A gallon of water weighs about eight pounds, so on a three-day trip, each hiker would have to carry at least twenty-four pounds of water.

■ Don't save weight by leaving water at home; instead abandon extra equipment like binoculars, and camera equipment.

■ Alternatively, shop for a superlight tent and sleeping bag. Many nights in the desert, all you really want around you is a good nylon barrier between you and the creepy crawlies.

■ Although the lack of water presents the biggest challenge for the hiker in the desert, sunshine also requires special preparation and planning. Two pieces of equipment that might be optional elsewhere are essential here—sunglasses and sunscreen.

■ Pay attention to types of clothing you pick; go light and white. Use cotton whenever possible.

■ Take advantage of the early morning in the desert—the best time of day for wildlife, temperature, and pictures, although the evening can be nice also.

■ For more information on desert backpacking, read *Desert Hiking Tips* by Bruce Grubbs.

Mountain Lion Awareness

■ Mountain lions are rarely seen, but when they are it is often a dangerous situation. The best advice is to avoid hiking, running, or biking alone in lion country. For more information read *Lion Sense* by Steven Torres.

■ If attacked, fight back. Most attacks can be thwarted by aggressive response.

■ Be especially mindful of small children in lion country. Keep them close and in sight.

■ Keep small dogs on a leash or leave them at home. Small pets are frequent targets of suburban mountain lions.

■ Stay clear of all wild animals—mountain lions, elk, moose, bison, bears, gators, and the like—for both your benefit and theirs. Animal-human encounters often scare both and lead wild animals to waste calories running from the perceived threat—calories they may need to store to make it through the winter.

Bear Awareness

■ The bear essentials:
  • Knowledge is the best defense.
  • There is no substitute for being alert.
  • Hike with a large group, and stay together.

- Do not hike alone in bear country.
- Stay on the trail.
- Hike in the middle of the day.
- Make lots of noise while hiking.
- Never approach a bear.
- Females with cubs are very dangerous.
- Stay away from carcasses.
- Keep separate sleeping and cooking areas.
- Sleep in a tent.
- Cook just the right amount of food, and eat it all.
- Store food and garbage out of reach of bears.
- Never feed bears.
- Keep food odors out of the tent.
- Leave the campsite cleaner than you found it.
- Leave no food rewards for bears.
- Report all bear sightings to a ranger.

■ Use your knowledge of bear habitat and habits: Be especially alert in areas most likely to be frequented by bears. This includes areas such as avalanche chutes, berry patches, streams, stands of whitebark pine, and high-wind or high-noise areas.

■ There is safety in numbers: There have been very few instances where a large group has had an encounter with a bear.

■ Be sure to hang your pack out of reach of bears anytime you leave it, even for a short side trip. It keeps the squirrels and marmots out of it, too. Leaving an unsecured pack violates backcountry regulations in some national parks.

Zero-Impact Backpacking

■ Going into the wilderness is like visiting a famous museum. If everybody going through a museum left one little mark, the contents of the museum would quickly be destroyed, and of what value is a big building full of trashed art? The same goes for a pristine wilderness such as the backcountry, which is as magnificent as any masterpiece by any artist. If we all left just one little mark on the landscape, the wilderness would soon be despoiled.

■ A wilderness can accommodate human use as long as everybody behaves. However, a few thoughtless or uninformed visitors can ruin it for everybody who follows. All wilderness users have a responsibility to know and follow the rules of zero-impact camping. Canoeists can look behind the canoe and see no trace of their passing. Hikers, mountain bikers, horse packers, and four-wheelers should have the same goal. Enjoy the wilderness, but don't leave any trace of your visit.

■ The philosophy of zero-impact backpacking in three sentences:
  • Leave with everything you brought with you.
  • Leave no trace of your visit.

• Leave everything you find where you found it.

■ Most of us know better than to litter in or out of the wilderness. Be sure you leave nothing, regardless of how small it is, along the trail or at the campsite. Pack out everything, including orange peels, flip tops, cigarette butts, and gum wrappers. Also pick up any trash that others have left behind.

■ Carry a readily available plastic bag for trash you encounter on the trail. —*Polly Burke*

■ Don't just roll a rock on your business because you are too lazy to dig a hole! Chances are someone or something will disturb the rock and expose your excrement to the next hiker.

■ Zero-impact backpacking, step by step:
  • Follow the main trail.
  • Avoid cutting switchbacks and walking on vegetation beside the trail.
  • Don't pick up rocks, antlers, or wildflowers. The next person wants to see them, too, and collecting such souvenirs is often illegal.
  • Remember, sound travels easily to the other side of a lake.
  • Be courteous.
  • Carry a lightweight trowel to bury human waste, and pack out used toilet paper. Keep human waste at least 200 feet from any water source.

- Strictly follow the pack-in/pack-out rule. If you carry something into the backcountry, consume it or carry it out.

■ After practicing these principles, put your ear to the ground in the wilderness and listen carefully. Thousands of people coming behind you are thanking you for your courtesy and good sense.

■ On your way to the trailhead, stay on the designated road. Do not veer off-road just to miss a small puddle or rock; practice low-impact driving, too.

Helping Management Agencies

■ For your safety and the safety of other wilderness travelers, you should report all trail dangers to the local ranger district. This includes any wild animal confrontations, bears eating garbage, habituated deer, dangerous fords, washed-out trails, and illegal human activity. It is up to us to make managing public lands easy for agencies by obeying local regulations, picking up garbage along the trail, and practicing low-impact ethics. Doing these things will ensure that our children get to see the same wild lands we did, untrammeled and pristine.

Backpacking with Children

■ Backpack only within a half day's walk of the car in case you need to bail.

■ The amount of time you backpack might drop substantially after you have kids, but the quality of the life-sharing experience will greatly increase.

■ When you take your kids backpacking, proper clothing for them is as important as any item in your pack.

■ Don't forget your s'more stuff (chocolate bars, graham crackers, and marshmallows). Put your graham crackers in a hard plastic container; no one likes crumbs.

Backpacking Checklists

■ Probably the best way to make sure you have everything you need before a trip is to have a checklist. The following appendix includes a list of essential gear for backpacking and our personal list of what we really carry.

■ Keep weight in mind during all your trip planning.

■ Consider these checklists as guides only; you should carefully consider each item you take. All of these checklists are designed for groups of three people; hiking solo is not recommended.

■ Remember to keep extra food, water, and clothing in the car.

■ The best place to store your checklist is in the top pocket of your pack so that you can take notes for the next time. —*Bill Hunger*

■ Although standardized checklists are helpful, each person should develop his or her own personalized checklist derived from experience hiking in different seasons and trip duration. Keep good notes during each trip of what works and what doesn't work for you in order to refine your personal pretrip checklist. —*Bill Cunningham*

BACKPACKING CHECKLISTS

Basic Checklist

The list below represents a basic checklist for a three-day, two-night backpack for three people. If you go by yourself, you will need to shave off a few pounds, most likely with a lighter tent and less cookware. The checklist starts with items that all parties should carry, and then adds in their percentage of the group's weight if the group items are divided equally. Food is not listed as a group item, because each person would carry the same amount of food with or without a group. The list includes articles of clothing you wear on the first day and hence have to carry the rest of the trip.

Individual Items	Weight (oz.)
❏ One-liter water bottle (full of water, two if water is scarce or weather is hot)	36
❏ Lightweight backpack (internal frame, doubles as partial emergency sleeping shell)	72
❏ Synthetic sleeping bag (20 degree Fahrenheit rating, in a garbage bag and stuffed into a stuff sack)	61
❏ Pack fly or poncho (to cover pack while hiking and while breaking camp; can also be used as a ground cloth)	12
❏ Foam sleeping pad	9
❏ Heavy-duty garbage bags	6

Clothing

❏ Baggy hiking shorts	6
❏ Hiking hat (with brim)	3
❏ Knit hat (wool or synthetic)	4

❏ Trail hiking shoes	48
❏ Polypropylene long underwear (tops and bottoms)	12
❏ Underwear (at least two sets)	12
❏ Rain pants	22
❏ Waterproof or rubberized rain jacket	36
❏ Wool or synthetic gloves	2
❏ Wool or synthetic socks (1 pair)	8
❏ Wool sweater (or synthetic insulated jacket)	22
❏ Cotton socks (2 pair)	12

Survival Kit

❏ Candle	1
❏ Cigarette lighters (2, in waterproof wrapper)	2
❏ Compass with signal mirror	2
❏ Emergency fire starter in film case	1.5
❏ Emergency food bars (2)	5
❏ Iodine tablets (backup)	1.5
❏ Matches (with strike strip in waterproof container)	1.2
❏ Plastic whistle	0.8
❏ Space blanket	2
❏ Pocket knife	3.5

Top of Pack (Survival/Safety Items Continued)

❏ Bug repellent in sealed bag	2
❏ Duct tape (partial roll on pencil)	1
❏ Extra batteries (4 AA)	4
❏ Extra bulbs in film case	2
❏ Head lamp (with fresh batteries)	8.5
❏ Keys (attached to inside of pack)	3
❏ Map (each member of group should have a copy)	3.5
❏ Money, credit card, driver's license	2
❏ Sunglasses (in breakproof case)	3
❏ Sunscreen	2
❏ Plastic trowel and toilet paper and any needed feminine hygiene products	10

| ❏ Waterproof journal and pencil | 4 |
| ❏ Toothbrush and toothpaste | 4 |

Food (per person)	85 oz. total
❏ Drink bag: 6 tea bags, 3 apple cider packets, 6 soup packets, 5 lemon-flavor packets	10
❏ Snacks/breakfast: 6 breakfast bars, 2 cups trail mix, bag of almonds, 3 boxes raisins	37
❏ Meal bag 1: baguette and 12 oz. sharp cheddar cheese	23
❏ Meal bag 2: noodles-and-sauce or rice-and-sauce dinners	12
❏ Insulated plastic cup with lid	3
❏ Plastic spoon and fork	1.5
Weight of Individual Items	**539 oz. (33.7 lbs.)**

Group Items	**Weight (oz.)**
❏ Camp stove (with cigarette lighter)	24
❏ Fuel bottle (full of gas, 32 oz., may vary with fuel efficiency of stove)	29
❏ Pans (2 pans, lids, handles)	21
❏ Pepper spray (in bear country)	16
❏ 50 feet of cord	4
❏ Tent (three-person)	91
❏ Water filter (carry backup iodine in personal survival kit)	19
❏ Permit (if required)	0.1

First-aid Kit	
❏ Ace bandage	2.5
❏ Adhesive bandages	1.5
❏ Adhesive tape (1 roll)	3
❏ Antibiotic ointment packets (or small tube of Neosporin)	0.5
❏ Cravat (triangular bandage)	1.8

❑ Gauze pads (four, 4" x 4")	1.6
❑ Gauze roll	2
❑ Medications (laxative, antidiarrhea, allergy, aspirin, 2 ibuprofen)	2
❑ Nonadhesive bandage (for burns)	0.5
❑ Nylon bag	4
❑ Rubber/vinyl gloves (2 pair)	1.4
❑ Safety pins	0.5
❑ Scissors	3
❑ Tweezers (forceps)	0.5
❑ Wound-closure strips	0.5
❑ Moleskin or molefoam pieces	2
Weight of Group Items	**231.4 (77.1 oz. per person)**
Weight per Person	**616.1 oz. (38.5 lbs.)**

NOTE: If you have any special conditions or allergies (such as to bee stings), you should consult with your physician before taking a backpacking trip. If you are allergic to bee stings, carry an anaphylaxis emergency kit. If you are diabetic, be sure to include sufficient insulin and glucose paste for emergencies. If you are traveling in snake country, be sure to carry a snakebite kit. For more information on wilderness first aid, the authors recommend *Wilderness First Aid* by Gilbert Preston, M.D.

WHAT'S REALLY IN BILL'S BACKPACK

Attached on the Outside of Pack

- ❏ Leatherman tool
- ❏ Bear spray
- ❏ Carabiner
- ❏ Sleeping pad
- ❏ Fly rod and reel outfit
- ❏ Camera in ziplock bag in carrying case attached to shoulder strap
- ❏ Pack fly

Top Pocket

- ❏ Binoculars in ziplock bag
- ❏ Notebook and two pens in ziplock bag
- ❏ Toilet paper and trowel in ziplock bag
- ❏ Car keys on safety clip
- ❏ Fishing license, credit card, cash (bills plus two quarters and a dime), and driver's license in ziplock bag
- ❏ Map (unless it's in my pocket)
- ❏ Camera in ziplock bag
- ❏ Cell phone in ziplock bag (for emergencies only, i.e., always turned off)
- ❏ Mosquito head net
- ❏ Insect repellent
- ❏ Extra glasses

Back Pockets

❑ Filter

❑ Water bottle

Main Pocket

❑ Stove*

❑ Gas*

❑ Two cooking pans* (inside pans: matches in waterproof bottle with starter strip, scrubby, and tiny funnel

❑ Emergency kit—compass with built-in signal mirror, compass instructions, emergency fishing gear, candle, two cigarette lighters, fire starter, whistle, two small energy bars, a few pieces of hard candy, iodine tablets, small waterproof notebook and pencil, rock chalk, and emergency space blanket

❑ First-aid kit—small off-the-shelf kit with these additions: extra moleskin, ibuprofen, Percocet (superstrong prescription painkiller), hay fever/allergy treatment pills, Pepto-Bismol, and Neosporin

❑ Head lamp

❑ Bear hanging bag with attached cord

❑ Insulated mug

❑ Lightweight plastic bowl (so that I can eat and enjoy a hot drink at the same time)

❑ Paper towels*

- ❏ "Biz bag" containing utensils, vitamins, salt, pepper, dried onions, toothbrush, toothpaste, dental floss, comb, and matches in waterproof container (old vitamin bottle) with starter strip
- ❏ Food* split into three different-color stuff sacks:
  - • Drinks (tea, Cup-a-Soup, apple cider, lemonade, and hot chocolate)
  - • Meals (rice or pasta dinners, soup, bread and cheese, oatmeal, granola, and dried milk)
  - • Snacks (gorp, raisins, energy bars, nuts, jerky, and granola bars)
- ❏ Utility bag containing extra batteries (for head lamp and camera), extra garbage and ziplock bags, two lightweight tent stakes, coffee filters, duct tape, parachute cord, playing cards, coffee filters, pencil, and book
- ❏ Small fanny pack containing fly-fishing equipment

Bottom Pocket

- ❏ Sleeping bag in garbage bags
- ❏ Dry clothes in two garbage bags
- ❏ Extra clothes in garbage bags
- ❏ Tent and poles*
- ❏ Waterproof/windproof coat and rain pants

*Shared equipment that might be carried by somebody else (Bill hopes!)

WHAT'S REALLY IN RUSS'S BACKPACK

Overnight Equipment

❏ Strap tent, rolled in pad to outside; carry water filter, one water bottle, and bear spray on outside; bear spray on belt.

Body of Pack

❏ Four Outdoor Research waterproof stuff sacks, different colors—one designated for food-related items, one for emergency clothing

❏ Osprey Advent backpack (4 lbs., 8 oz.)

❏ Walrus Micro-Swift tent (1-person)

❏ North Face 0-Degree down sleeping bag (I prefer down because it is light for the amount of warmth; however, modern synthetic bags are also a good choice and perform better when wet. Remember to put a garbage bag inside your stuff sack and stuff your sleeping bag into it to prevent a wet bag. I also use one of my waterproof stuff sacks for my bag.)

❏ Foam sleeping pad (a long simple foam pad; a heavy Therma-Lounger is better for the river when weight is not an issue)

❏ Glacier Wilderness Guides coffee cup, old school with slogan, "You won't know if you don't go!"

❏ Red Nalgene plastic 1-liter fuel bottle with internal spout

- ❏ Sigg small metal fuel bottle wrapped in duct tape (emergency-only extra fuel supply, nice to have in a wet snowstorm)
- ❏ Emergency clothing stuff sack (stocking cap, wool gloves, Capalyne underwear tops and bottoms)
- ❏ Bug nets (carry 8 total, with 1 or 2 in the top of my pack, can occasionally save the day!)
- ❏ Miscellaneous food stuff sacks (cheap, nonwaterproof)
- ❏ Cook kit in large MSR stuff stack, MSR pans—small pan and lid, large pan and lid, plastic forks, spoons (When I used to guide I carried a lightweight nonstick fry pan and soap, a scrubby, bleach, and a mesh screen for filtering chunks out of discarded dishwater—leave no chunks. If you can get away with it spacewise, it is nice to store your stove inside the pans; always have an extra cigarette lighter in there, too.)
- ❏ Peak 1 Stove (I have also used MSR Whisperlight and Optimus Expedition regularly. Whisperlights are hard to simmer on and harder to light correctly for most people. Optimus, at least the more reliable Optimus Expedition version, was very good but also very heavy for a stove and only fit for large-group cooking. Peak 1 has proven the most reliable, regular and easy to fix, of the stoves I have used, and my feet have straddled many hours of camp cooking.)

- ❑ Kelty lightweight nylon tarp (8 by 8 feet, with parachute cord attached to each grommet)
- ❑ Dana Design Gore-Tex pack fly *with hood* that covers head and back (Really, really nice to have the hood. Lots of pack flies cover your pack but don't cover the area between your pack and your back, where the water runs. In addition, hiking in full rain gear is often too hot, and a pack fly that extends out over your head allows you to make time without the on-and-off of rain gear. One of the best pieces of equipment I ever purchased.)
- ❑ Fifty feet of Spectra quarter-inch rope with carabiner (may want to pack bear-proof containers; may be required in some areas.)
- ❑ Overnight food (Annie's Bunny Pasta, Lipton Rice & Sauce, baguettes, sharp cheddar, summer sausage)
- ❑ Drink bag (hot cocoa, tea, instant oatmeal, Cup-a-Soup)
- ❑ Overnight clothing (fleece pants, fleece jacket, shorts, T-shirts, several pairs of socks)

Top of Pack
- ❑ Aviator playing cards
- ❑ Minitube of toothpaste, sawed-off toothbrush, floss, comb
- ❑ Blistex lip protection
- ❑ Unscented Cutter insect repellent
- ❑ Another bug net

- ❏ ziplock bag with a few baby wipes (a great way to maintain some semblance of sanity)
- ❏ Spare tent pole repair tubes
- ❏ Coleman Peak 1 stove repair kit (mostly parts for pump)
- ❏ Extra strap and extra quick-release buckle
- ❏ Walrus tent repair instructions
- ❏ Fishing regulations
- ❏ Extra strap
- ❏ Very old emergency Cliff Bar (probably should have been thrown out awhile ago)
- ❏ Miscellaneous garbage
- ❏ Extra tent stakes
- ❏ Ben's 100 DEET
- ❏ Two dollars
- ❏ More garbage
- ❏ Sight Savers, lens cleaners
- ❏ Extra batteries
- ❏ Two quarters

Everyday Items

Stuff transferred out of daypack into backpack for overnight trips; start of day hike checklist portion. I prefer a Kelty traditional backpack.

Top of Pack
- ❏ USGS maps
- ❏ Pencil and paper

- ❏ Extra ziplock bag
- ❏ Toilet paper (partial roll)
- ❏ Trowel
- ❏ Purrell hand sanitizer (I wish I had invented this!)
- ❏ Boat/shuttle schedules
- ❏ Off insect repellent
- ❏ Survival Kit (Keep mesh bag full of survival kit for portability into other outdoor gear.)
- ❏ Princeton head lamp, good batteries in it
- ❏ Extra batteries
- ❏ Extra lightbulb taped in a film canister
- ❏ Whistle
- ❏ Survival kit with matches in it (regular matches with strike strip inside)
- ❏ Brunton compass
- ❏ Small signal mirror
- ❏ Waterproof propane lighter and blocks of artificial fire-starting material wrapped in plastic in a ziplock bag with lighter (excellent thing to carry in your lifejacket for you river folk, in the other pocket from your flip/rescue line)
- ❏ Leatherman tool
- ❏ Yellow flagging
- ❏ Buck knife
- ❏ Several cigarette lighters

Body of Pack and Outside

- ❑ MSR Water Works water filter, with small container of bleach, small container of lube for pump (Remember iodine in emergency kit.)
- ❑ Two one-liter bottles of water (one Thermoplastic Nalgene bottle that can withstand hot liquids; nice for emergency warming situations)
- ❑ Fleece gloves
- ❑ Polartec long-sleeve shirt
- ❑ Marmot synthetic long underwear
- ❑ Extensive first-aid kit (I still carry my "group" first-aid kit, which is a bit of overkill.)
- ❑ Specialized fleece vest
- ❑ Knit watch cap (wool hat)
- ❑ Gore-Tex rain jacket, rain pants, and hat
- ❑ Counter Assault pepper spray
- ❑ Plano fishing fanny pack (Minimalist fishing contents, but remember your reel and two separate boxes of flies so that if you drop one downriver you still have another stash to fish with.)
- ❑ St. Croix 4-piece 4-weight fly rod (Breaks down into four pieces with reel on. You also can leave it rigged if you are careful, ready to fish out of the zippered case.)

NOTE: Consider cookware, stove, fuel, food, first-aid kit, tent, and tarp as group items for sharing weight.

Post-trip Checklist

Once you get to the trailhead and change clothes, stop at a pizza place, and grab a cold beverage, don't forget your post-trip duties. It is in your best interest to do a little post-trip maintenance, especially if your trip has been a dirty one. Probably the most important thing you can do to preserve your gear is to make sure it is clean and dry before storing it.

❑ Call or notify those you left word with of your itinerary so that they know you got back safely and won't call for a massive search. An unwanted search for someone who is not lost is costly—and embarrassing.

❑ For your safety and the safety of other wilderness travelers, you should report all trail dangers to the local ranger district.

❑ Clean all gear and repair any items damaged during the trip so that you're ready for the next trip.

❑ Take your sleeping bag out of the stuff sack and put it loosely in a storage bag.

❑ Dry out your tent, fly, and rain gear before storing.

❑ Dump your garbage, but don't fill trailhead garbage cans. Drive it in; drive it out.

❑ Replenish survival and first-aid items so that you don't forget them on the next trip.

FALCONGUIDES BY THE CONTRIBUTORS

Ron Adkison

Hiking Northern California, Hiking Southern California, Hiking Washington, Hiking Wyoming's Wind River Range, Hiking Grand Canyon National Park, Best Easy Day Hikes Grand Canyon, Wild Northern California, Best Easy Day Hikes Northern Sierra, Best Easy Day Hikes Southern Sierra, Hiking Grand Staircase–Escalante, Best Easy Day Hikes Grand Staircase–Escalante

Fred Barstad

A FalconGuide to Mount St. Helens, Hiking Oregon's Eagle Cap Wilderness, Hiking Mount St. Helens, Hiking Hells Canyon & Idaho's Seven Devils Wilderness, Hiking Washington's Mount Adams Country, Hiking Washington's Goat Rocks Country

Polly Burke

Hiking California's Desert Parks, Hiking New Mexico's Aldo Leopold Wilderness, Hiking New Mexico's Gila Wilderness, Best Easy Day Hikes Joshua Tree, Best Easy Day Hikes Death Valley, Best Easy Day Hikes Anza–Borrego

Bill Cunningham

Wild Montana, Hiking California's Desert Parks, Hiking New Mexico's Aldo Leopold Wilderness, Hiking New Mexico's Gila Wilderness, Best Easy Day Hikes Joshua Tree, Best Easy Day Hikes Death Valley, Best Easy Day Hikes Anza–Borrego

Bert and Jane Gildart

Hiking South Dakota's Black Hills Country, Best Easy Day Hikes Shenandoah National Park, Hiking Shenandoah National Park, A FalconGuide to Dinosaur National Monument, A FalconGuide to Death Valley National Park

Bruce Grubbs

Hiking Great Basin National Park, Hiking Nevada, Hiking Northern Arizona, Using GPS, Desert Hiking Tips, Best Easy Day Hikes Flagstaff, Best Easy Day Hikes Sedona, Camping Arizona, Mountain Biking Phoenix

Will Harmon

Leave No Trace, Wild Country Companion, Mountain Biking Helena

Bill Hunger

Hiking Wyoming

Donna Ikenberry

Hiking Colorado's Weminuche and South San Juan Wilderness Area, Camping Utah, Wild Colorado

Rhonda and George Ostertag

Hiking Pennsylvania, Hiking New York, Hiking Southern New England, Camping Oregon

Gilbert Preston, M.D.

Wilderness First Aid